USBORNE

24 Hours
in a Zoo

Lan Cook

Illustrated by Stacey Thomas

Designed by Tom Ashton-Booth

Consultant: Kirsten Wicks

Kirsten Wicks works for Chester Zoo – the most visited zoo in the UK and
a world-leading conservation and education charity committed to preventing
extinction and raising awareness of key conservation challenges worldwide.

Usborne Quicklinks

For links to websites and videos where you can see zoo
animals up close and meet the people who look after them,
go to usborne.com/Quicklinks and type in the title of this book.

Here are some of the things you can do at
the websites we recommend:

- Take a virtual tour of a zoo
- Meet the endangered mountain chicken frog
- See what goes on after dark in a nocturnal house
- Visit a zoo hospital and see how vets help their animal patients
- Watch animal enrichment in action
- Discover how much food a zoo needs

Look out for me from page 18
onwards. I go on my own day
out exploring the zoo!

CONTENTS

The sun has risen on a warm summer morning at the zoo.

The animals are waking up...

...their calls ring out across the park.

7 a.m. In a secluded corner of the zoo...

STAFF HOUSING

...OOOOOOOoUUUUUHHHH

Yes! Today's the day.

...OOHHWWWwwHHHHHRRRRRR

Morning, Aunt Ari!

Morning, Tai. Ready to see what it's like to be a zookeeper?

SO ready! I've been waiting for this all year.

Great! Have some breakfast and we'll head out.

What's in the zoo...

1 Poo plant
2 Keeper HQ
3 Vet's office
4 Food prep
5 Red pandas & echidnas
6 *COMING SOON*
7 Spectacled bears
8 Sun bears
9 Colombian red howler monkeys
10 Tropical house

11 Amphibian nursery
12 Sumatran tigers
13 Flamingo lake
14 Jaguars
15 Giant anteater & lowland tapirs
16 Rainforest aviary
17 Bird nursery
18 Spotted hyenas
19 Nocturnal house
20 Aquarium

21 Chimpanzees
22 Aardvarks
23 Maned wolves
24 Sumatran orangutans
25 African lions
26 Giraffes
27 Meerkats
28 Otters
29 Hippos
30 African elephants

It's going to be a hot day. Want to help me make some frozen treats for the bears and red pandas later?

How about I cut up the fruits and veggies, and you weigh and put it into the containers to freeze.

In hot weather, even animals that are used to high temperatures need some help to keep cool.

I'm on it!

Different types of food are prepared in separate areas. This keeps everything hygienic.

Hi, Kit. What are you making today?

Oh, these are vegetable kebabs for the Galapagos tortoises.

I just thread the veggies onto these ropes to hang up. It really gets the tortoises moving.

When their food is hung up like this, tortoises have to push up with their front legs and extend their necks to reach it.

Galapagos giant tortoise

13

Keeping things interesting

Zoos give animals activities that encourage them to interact with their surroundings in a similar way to their wild counterparts. These activities are known as enrichment, and there are five main types...

Food

The most widely used form of enrichment encourages animals to search for food.

Some food is scattered.

Sun bear

Some food is smeared on things.

Some food is hidden.

Sumatran tiger

CRUNCH

Chimpanzees

Sensory

Sensory enrichment is designed to stimulate the five senses.

Sumatran orangutans

Lookout platforms give animals a wide view.

CRUNCH CRUNCH

Providing items – such as mounds of dried leaves – lets animals experience new textures.

New smells keep animals mentally and physically alert. Big cats seem to love sniffing out certain colognes.

African lion

RUB

RUB

Mental

Many animals are highly intelligent. Setting them challenges and puzzles helps give them the mental exercise they need.

With puzzle feeders, animals such as parrots and octopuses have to think carefully about how they can get at their food.

In the wild, black palm cockatoos are the only animals known to make their own tools to make music.

Octopuses are one of the world's most intelligent species.

Social

Social interaction is an important part of many animals' lives.

Lowland tapir

Giant anteater

Animals are often housed with species that they would share space with in the wild.

Habitat

Zoo habitats are designed with each animal's natural instincts in mind.

Two-toed sloth

Climbing frames, ropes, perches, swings, high platforms, hammocks and more all encourage animals to behave as they would in the wild.

Private spaces allow animals to spend time away from each other and the public.

Meerkats

Ha! Tai, you sound just as excited as I feel. It is, and they'll be here during the night...

Is that the habitat for the new animals?

Are they arriving soon?

...between one and two a.m. if everything runs on schedule.

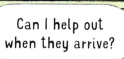

Can I help out when they arrive?

Hmm, we'll see. For now, let's take this food to the bears.

Keepers only enter habitats of large animals when the animals are safely inside an inner enclosure.

Habitats have double-door systems for safety. One door must always be closed before the other is opened.

Food for bears is hidden in trees and up climbing frames.

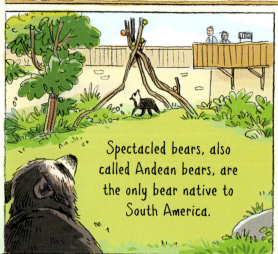

Spectacled bears, also called Andean bears, are the only bear native to South America.

Each bear has unique markings on its face and chest.

These bears have extremely sensitive noses. They can smell ripe fruit from many miles away.

Let's head over to the sun bears and give them their treat!

Wanna see who can throw their watermelon the furthest?

Challenge... accepted.

Sun bears are the smallest bear species. They are native to the tropical forests of Southeast Asia.

To communicate, they copy each others' facial expressions. They are the only species apart from primates and dogs known to do this.

Like most bears, sun bears are omnivores. This means they eat all sorts – including insects, seeds, nuts, fruit and small animals.

Hey, Tai! I've come to take you to the frog nursery with me. You ready?

Definitely! I've always wanted to see inside there! See you later, Aunt Ari!

Have fun! It's on to cleaning for me.

Well, first it was habitat loss, then a volcanic eruption...

...but now they're threatened by a highly infectious disease called chytridiomycosis.

An amphibian apocalypse

Chytridiomycosis *(kai-trid-ee-oh-my-co-sis)* is caused by two types of chytrid fungus. It's thought to be one of the main threats to amphibian species around the world.

Chytrid fungus spores

Around half of all known amphibian species could become extinct – die out – but for some, it's already too late.

To safeguard remaining species, some have been removed from the wild and kept in a safe, fungus-free environment.

After making sure they're not infected, many of these endangered species are bred in captivity to keep a population going.

Researchers have successfully treated the disease in captivity. Now, zoos and scientists around the world are working together to find a way to prevent and cure the disease on a large scale in the wild.

Keepers often carefully remove the eggs to incubate them. That means keeping them warm and safe until they start to hatch.

When the time is right, we introduce the hatching tadpoles into a water tank. If it's done too soon the tadpoles could drown.

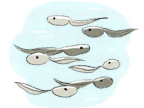

As the tadpoles develop, we move them from the water...

... to a tank with shallow water and land in it...

...then finally, they move in with their parents.

Wow! It sounds like a long process.

Hana, what's that speaker in with the frogs for?

Ah well...

It can be. Timings are crucial.

...frogs in zoos lose their "accent" over time. Their calls start to sound different from those in the wild.

When the frogs are ready to be reintroduced to the wild, we want them to speak the local language. So...

...we play them recordings of wild golden mantellas so they learn a Madagascan accent.

CHIRP CHIRP
CHIRP
CHIRP
CHIRP
CHIRP
CHIRP CHIRP

Oh! I'm supposed to be helping move the anaconda for her health check!

Tai, do you want to watch from a distance?

Do I want to see how you move a giant snake? Definitely!

How come she needs a health check?

She's lost her appetite recently. We just want to make sure there's nothing serious going on.

Brunhilda! Where... Brunhilda?!

PAP   PAP

10 a.m. In the tropical house...

Thanks for coming everyone. So let's remember to treat Annie with respect. As a category one animal she's one of our most dangerous creatures.

Zoos rank animals according to how dangerous they are. Category one animals include big cats, wolves, rhinos, elephants and great apes.

Some snakes have heat vision. This is how things look through Annie's eyes.

Green anacondas live in the swamps, marshes and slow-moving streams of the South American rainforests. They are the heaviest and one of the longest species of snake.

Let's lay her down over here. All together now.

Oh, her scales are *so* smooth!

Keep a tight hold of her, I'll check her over for parasites first.

The snake's mouth is held open carefully to keep the snake and the vet from getting hurt.

Blood samples can be used to check blood sugar levels, diseases, and problems with internal organs such as the liver or kidneys

Ok. Let's put her in the tub and take her for an X-ray so we can look at what's going on inside her.

They can only X-ray around 43cm (17in) at a time, so it is done in multiple sections.

Snakes must be laid out straight to make sure X-ray photographs are clear.

Whew! That was intense. I'll be right back, I'm going to open the tropical house back up to the public.

New Guinea crocodiles

Now extinct, the titanoboa lived 60 million years ago in what is now Colombia, South America.

Titanoboa (Life-size model)

It's the biggest snake that ever lived – so big, its diet included crocodiles.

Hey, Tai! Good morning so far?

It's been amazing! I was just imagining what it would be like to give one of these a health check!

Ha! I think I'll stick with my bears. Follow me. We're going to see something very special...

OOH!

Colombian red howler monkeys

KSSSHHH

KSSSHHH

Amphibians here. Message for Mr. McQueen. Please meet the mountain chicken at home.

Translation: *This is the amphibian section. We have an escaped mountain chicken frog. Meet at the amphibian nursery so we can start looking.*

Sumatran tigers

Andean flamingos

KSSSHHH

KSSSHHH

Zookeepers use walkie talkies to communicate with each other. If an animal escapes, keepers speak in code so guests at the zoo don't panic.

KSSSHHH

Hi, you two!

Did you hear about the frog over the walkie talkies?!

We did! We'll all have to keep an eye out.

I'm sure they'll find it quickly! C'mon, shall we go in? Try to stay really quiet.

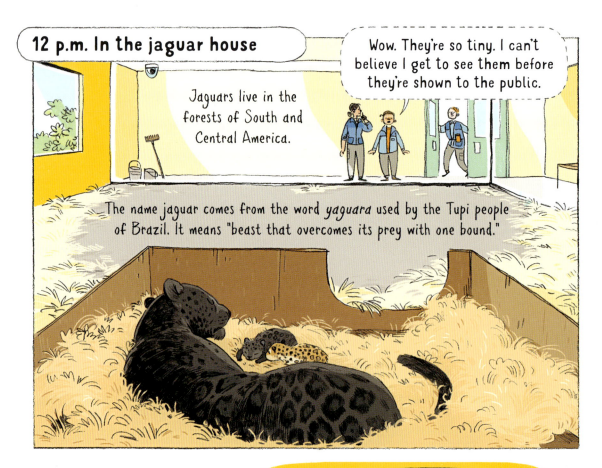

Wow. They're so tiny. I can't believe I get to see them before they're shown to the public.

Jaguars live in the forests of South and Central America.

The name jaguar comes from the word *yaguara* used by the Tupi people of Brazil. It means "beast that overcomes its prey with one bound."

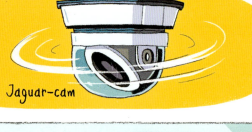

Let's head through. We can watch Itztli and the cubs on the cameras while we eat lunch.

Jaguar-cam

How come Itztli and one of the cubs have black fur when jaguars are usually golden with black markings?

Ah, they're what's called melanistic.

Melanism

Melanism occurs when an animal has increased levels of very dark pigment called melanin in its skin, hair, scales or feathers.

Birds, reptiles, amphibians, mammals and insects can all be melanistic, but it's rare in fish.

Melanism can give animals an advantage. It can help camouflage them, making them less visible to predators or prey. This is known as adaptive melanism.

Around 10% of wild jaguars are melanistic.

In most black jaguars or leopards it is still possible to see their markings in certain lights.

Caring for Kakapo

Kakapo are flightless parrots native to New Zealand. Around 200 years ago, non-native cats, dogs and rats were introduced to the islands and hunted kakapo almost to extinction. In 1991, there were only 51 living individuals.

To help their numbers recover, all wild kakapo have been moved to islands free from predators.

Kakapo* means "night parrot" in the language of New Zealand's Māori people.

All the birds are given yearly health checks and supplementary food at feeding stations.

Some kakapo are very inquisitive and have little fear of humans or other animals. This is because they evolved with no land-based predators.

How come you're feeding the chicks? What happened to their mother?

She's fine! Unfortunately these little guys are here either because they're ill or injured. But they're doing well!

Because there are so few of them, all kakapo are given names.

Hi, I'm Tītapu.

*In modern Māori, kakapo is written kākāpō.

Ah, perfect timing! The food's ready.

Oh, why's it so warm!

The mothers part-digest the food before feeding it to their chicks. So we heat the food to kakapo body temperature.

Kakapo body temperature is 43°C (109°F).

So, what are we feeding them here?

GRAAAK!

GRAAAK!

GRAAAK!

It's a special liquid formula. When the mother feeds them, their food contains her saliva and gut bacteria...

...so we add acidophilus bacteria to the formula. This helps with digestion and keeps the chicks healthy.

Do you hand rear animals often?

Only when absolutely necessary. Whatever the species, it's best if animals can stay with their parents.

GRAAAK!

GRAAAK!

Most hand-reared kakapo chicks are looked after at a special facility, but those that are ill often come to us for medical care.

At around a hundred days old, hand-reared kakapo are returned to their islands to live in the wild. This ensures they don't "imprint" or become attached to humans and lose interest in other kakapo.

With any endangered species we want to make sure as many survive as possible.

Kakapo became endangered because of humans. Now it's up to us to make sure they don't become extinct.

Keepers in disguise

It's usually better for animals to raise their own young. But sometimes, this isn't possible. To make sure hand-reared animals don't become tame – especially those that will be returned to the wild – keepers sometimes disguise themselves to look like the animals' parent.

Glove puppets

Glove puppets are used at feeding time. They imitate the markings and look of adult birds.

Food is often given with tweezers.

Javan green magpie chick

Models

Keepers at some zoos wear helmets made to look like adult birds.

Northern bald ibis chicks

Beekeeping suit used as a disguise

Disguises

Sometimes keepers wear full disguises. This lets them teach young birds how to search for food and socialize with others without becoming familiar with humans.

Eurasian crane chick

2 p.m. Rico's appointment

Oh! We're due at the vet's office for Rico the toucan's appointment.

KSSHH KSSHH

Mr. McQueen to the hothouse. Repeat, Mr. McQueen to the hothouse.

Translation: The mountain chicken frog may have been spotted in the rainforest aviary.

I hope he'll feel so much better with this.

Oh no! We missed the fitting!

Oookay Rico. That looks pretty secure. You'll be the fanciest keel-billed toucan around!

Before he came to us, Rico had a terrible accident and lost most of his upper beak.

Wait... so is that... a *prosthetic* beak?

It is! Thanks to modern technology and a group of vets and engineers we can give him a new lease of life.

Toucans' beaks are made from keratin – the same stuff as our fingernails.

With a damaged beak, Rico would have struggled to sing, clean and feed himself. Toucans also rely on their beaks to regulate their body temperature.

Animal prosthetics

Over the years, all sorts of artificial body parts have been created to help injured and disabled animals.

Yu Chan the loggerhead turtle has rubber flippers.

Mr. Stubbs the alligator has a tail made from silicone.

Fred the tortoise has a 3-D printed shell made from corn-based plastic.

Asian elephant Motola has a leg made from steel, plastic and elastomer.

Short-beaked echidna

You'll see him in the penguin habitat. Which is your next stop today. Let's head there now, through the aquarium.

Green sea turtle

Helping sea turtles clean their shells keeps them healthy, and the turtles really seem to like it.

Blue-green chromis

Firefish

Azure damsel

Longnose hawkfish

Maroon clownfish

Green face wrasse

Mandarin goby

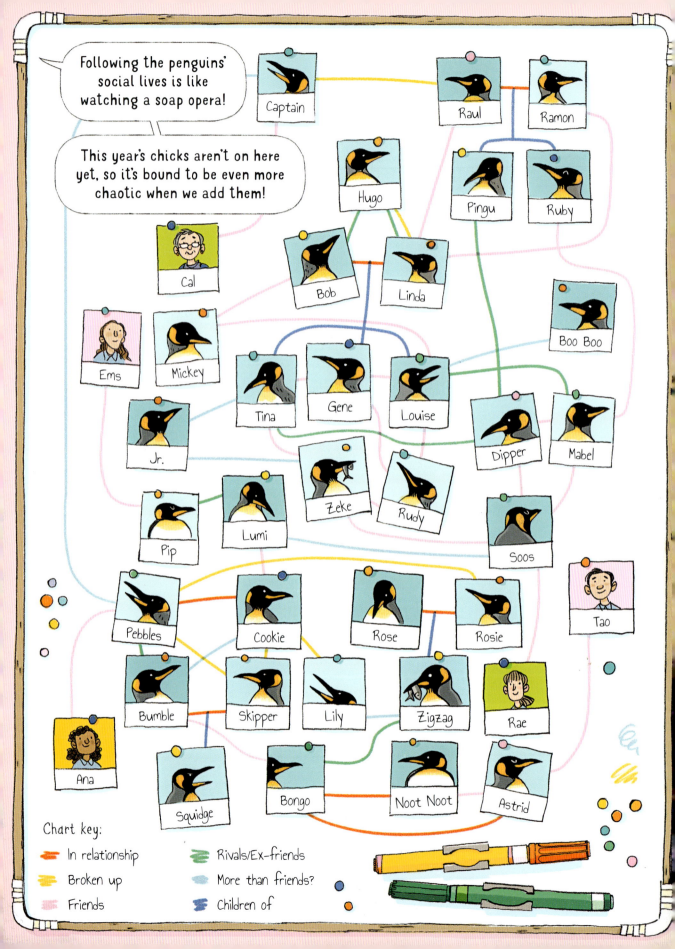

The nocturnal house...

Tai, before we go in, how are you with bats?

There's no pressure. We don't have to go in if you don't want to.

No, I'm ready. Let's do this!

I used to be the same y'know...

What, scared of bats? Really?

Errrm, well... they kind of scare me a bit actually. But I'm going to be brave!

Nocturnal houses use a system called "reverse lighting." That creates nighttime conditions during the day.

How did you end up looking after them then?

My ma brought me here, and a keeper told me all about bats, and let me feed one that was being hand reared.

After that, I just wanted to learn everything I could about them.

Well, I'm determined to leave here liking bats, just like you did!

Fruit on strings

They probably are! Egyptian fruit bats actually speak to one another, and it turns out they argue... a lot!

SKREEEK

SKREEEK

SKREEEK

Haha, what do they argue about?

They tend to argue about four things...

...food...

...who sleeps where within a group...

...unwanted attention...

...and when another bat sits too close.

They adjust the sound of their calls too, depending on who they're speaking to.

So, a bit like when we humans change our tone of voice?

SKREEEK

SKREEEK

SKREEEK

SKREEEK

SKREEEK

SKREEEK

SKREEEK

SKREEEK

Exactly like that.

Feeling a little less scared of them now?

SKREEK

SKREEK

I am, actually. Maybe I could come back and help you feed them again soon?

Of course! After we've finished putting food out, let's visit the nocturnal desert habitats too.

6:30 p.m. Closing time...

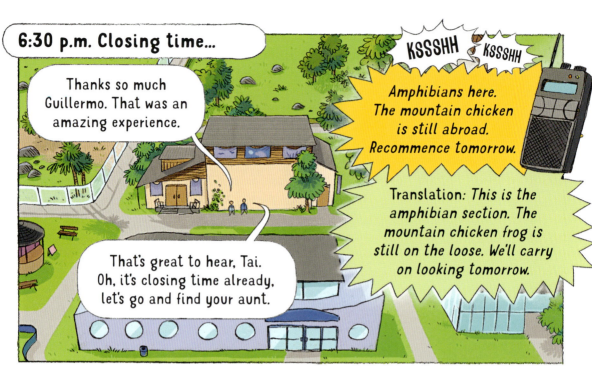

Thanks so much Guillermo. That was an amazing experience.

That's great to hear, Tai. Oh, it's closing time already, let's go and find your aunt.

KSSSHH KSSSHH

Amphibians here. The mountain chicken is still abroad. Recommence tomorrow.

Translation: *This is the amphibian section. The mountain chicken frog is still on the loose. We'll carry on looking tomorrow.*

Hi, Aunt Ari! I've had such a great day.

Fantastic! You can tell me all about it over dinner. But let's feed the red pandas theirs first.

In the wild, red pandas live in the eastern Himalayan mountains and southwestern China.

Despite their name, red pandas are not closely related to giant pandas.

The name panda comes from the Napali word "ponya" meaning "bamboo eater".

Lots of larger nighttime creatures like these don't live in nocturnal houses, but they are also more active from dusk, through the night until morning.

Spotted hyena OHHHWOOOP!

Hyenas are more closely related to cats than dogs.

OHHHWOOOP!

OHHHWOOOP!

Spotted hyenas live in family groups or "clans" that are matriarchies – led by the females.

Aardvark   Aardvark means "earth pig" in the Afrikaans language.

SNUFFLE

PRRRP

SNUFFLE

A single aardvark can eat around 50,000 insects in just one night.

Maned wolf

ROOORK!
ROOORK!

ROOORK!

Maned wolves are found in South America. When they sense danger, their mane stands on end.

Moving home

Transporting animals between zoos requires many months of careful planning.

Keepers from their new home often visit them before they move. This is so they can get to know each other.

If animals have to fly, they are placed in a temperature-controlled hold. Here, keepers and vets spend time with them, feed them and make sure they're happy and relaxed.

Animals are transported in custom-made crates or boxes. Before they travel, they are usually fed in the crate for a few weeks so they feel comfortable spending time in it.

Let's leave them for the rest of the night to settle in.

Will the public be able to see them right away?

No, we'll let them get used to their new home for a while first...

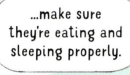

...make sure they're eating and sleeping properly.

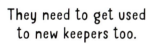

They need to get used to new keepers too.

C'mon, let's all get some rest. Li Ming, I'll show you to where you're staying.

Fantastic, thanks Ari, I think I've been up for almost 24 hours at this point.

In the morning I'll show you the panda observation room.

Coming, Tai?

Er, yep! Coming!

GLOSSARY

This glossary explains some of the words used in this book.
Words written in *italic* type have their own entries.

3-D printing – A way of making an object, layer-by-layer, using a computer-created design.

Bacteria – Microscopic living things that can be both harmful and helpful.

Biogas – A *renewable fuel* produced by *bacteria* breaking down natural material – often food waste or manure.

Chytridiomycosis – A highly-infectious disease in amphibians caused by a type of fungus.

Endangered *species* – A species of living thing that is in danger of becoming *extinct*.

Enrichment – Something that gives zoo animals mental and physical exercise.

Extinct – When an entire *species* dies out it becomes extinct.

Habitat – The environment where an animal or plant lives.

Hand rearing – When a human cares for a baby animal until it is able to look after itself.

Hybrid – The result of breeding two different *species* together.

Melanism – A high amount of a dark pigment called melanin found in skin, hair and feathers.

Methanization – The process by which waste is broken down to make *biogas*.

Parasite – An animal, plant or fungus that gets its food by living on or inside another animal or plant.

Prosthetic – A human-made body part created to replace one that is missing or damaged.

Renewable fuel – Fuel from a source that never runs out – for example, vegetable oil or food waste.

Species – A particular type of animal, plant or other living thing.

Target feeding – A way of feeding coral or other animals by putting food close to their mouths.

X-ray photograph – A picture of the inside of a person, animal or object.

INDEX

Chester Zoo

Chester Zoo is a world-leading conservation and education charity that's committed to preventing extinction and raising awareness of key conservation and environmental challenges. The zoo's 128-acre site in Chester, UK, is where this is made possible. The zoo works with more than 3,000 species globally, including 140 international animal conservation and breeding programmes, which are ensuring the survival of species on the very brink of extinction. This includes orangutans in Bornean rainforests, elephants and tigers in Indian grassland, lemurs and frogs in Malagasy forests, rare fish in Mexican lakes and various species in the UK.

Additional consultation by Dr. Andrew Digby, New Zealand Department of Conservation

Dr Andrew Digby is the Science Advisor for kākāpō and takahē (two large, flightless, endangered birds found only in New Zealand) with the Kākāpō Recovery Programme within the New Zealand Department of Conservation. He leads the scientific research upon which the conservation efforts are based.

Kākāpō Recovery Programme

The Kākāpō Recovery Programme was established in 1995 by New Zealand's Department of Conservation. Scientists, rangers and volunteers are working closely together with Māori iwi (tribes) to protect and grow the kākāpō population, and hope to eventually restore them to their former natural range.

Series editor: Ruth Brocklehurst
Series designer: Stephen Moncrieff

Additional design by Samantha Barrett

First published in 2023 by Usborne Publishing Limited,
83-85 Saffron Hill, London EC1N 8RT, United Kingdom. usborne.com